Catullus

THE POEMS OF
GAIUS VALERIUS CATULLUS:
Some English versions
by Roz Kaveney

Published by Sad Press in Bristol

September 2018

978-1-912802-22-7

Cover artwork by Rodolfo Clix

Set in Goudy Old Style

1. Dedication

Who gets first dibs on this cute little book
fresh from the printers all shiny and new?
Neil, you encouraged it. It goes to you.
You thought it good from your very first look.

That's quite impressive—you've written so much
history of Dreamland in so many volumes,
all of the endless in their Gothic costumes
all of the demons and angels and such.

So much you made up and so much is knowledge
picked up at random and stitched like a quilt
Reading your stories is fun without guilt.
Sex and adventure—and yet it's a college.

Anyway, here's my Catullus. Its pages
have filth, love and death. It is built for the ages.

2.

Sparrow my lover's delight,
playing then holding on tight
to her finger, and pecking at corn,
beak pecking her flesh like a thorn,
I'd prefer that I could make her smile
and lighten her gloom for a while
like you do. But at least she has you
and for now that will just have to do.

2B.

I throw these poems underneath her feet
that she might pause and read them as I chase
her. Otherwise I could not win this race,
from love would die. Poems like apples sweet
and firm and golden. Atalanta fell,
Diana's huntress, chaste, austere and fast.
But golden apples caught her eye at last,
twisted her ankle, turned her heart as well.

3.

Howl! Little boys with bows! You sweethearts! Cry!
Weep! All of you that walk in Venus' train!
The pretty, dingy sparrow has been slain
Lesbia loved. She'd rather lose an eye

she sometimes said. Chirrup pipip its song
close in her ear, in language she alone
could understand. Just as a mother's known
to some young girl, the sweet bird flew along

with her, sat in her lap. Without a breath
it flutters darkling never to come back.
Hell takes all things. Would not have felt the lack
of one small bird. So fuck you, greedy death,

Sparrow farewell! I must go wipe away
the tears my love sheds for you this dark day.

4.

Welcome aboard, she says. Trim swift and yare
won every race caught wind and made sails taut
oar slapping waves. Through winter storms she fought
the growling Northwind clawpawed spiteful bear
from every rock-tear coast armoured by speed
she grew tossed mountain wind that thrills through yet
each precious wood wrought firm cannot forget,
and grace she had as sapling and as seed.
Carried him tempest-battered, brings him home
traverse to green fields and this last blue lake,
prayed to the gods of storm his safety's sake,
now gentle wavelets topped with palest foam
rock as she chants her final sailor's hymn
to Castor saviour and his saviour twin.

5.

As long as we can go on living, dear,
my Lesbia, let's go on making love.
Old men may moan. A penny's worth above
the price of all their whinging, that is clear.

The sun can rise and set and rise again,
we only get one moment in the light
and then we fall asleep, and that good night,
is it forever. Let them fall like rain,

your kisses, on my lips, a thousand drops
two hundred more, and then a thousand more
a hundred next. They never get to bore,
each kiss is perfect, and it never stops,

kisses that no-one envies, for we say
we've no idea how much we've kissed today.

6.

There must be something wrong with your new girl
so you've not told me all about her. What's
the problem? Lank hair, squeaky voice or spots?
Is she some crazy tart? You're in a whirl,

not seeing straight. I've scrutinised your bed.
Empty, it's full of clues. Her cloying scent
on pillows. And your mattress is all bent,
it's squashed from fucking. All the springs are dead

on their last squeak. And you're shagged out as well,
so tired all the time. Clearly she's got
you round her finger, also up her twot.
And if you weren't ashamed of her, you'd tell.

So if you're quite convinced there's nothing wrong,
tell me so I can put it in a song.

7.

You've asked me, Lesbia, how many more
of our fond kisses might be just enough
to satisfy me. Asking is a bluff
but I'll give you my answer. On the shore

of Africa, line up each single grain
of sand, and count them individually.
The Pyramids' stone blocks, waves of each sea,
leaves on all trees, and every drop of rain—

still not enough. Count every quiet star
that gazes down through night at our bright love.
There aren't as many of them. From above
they know how very much in love we are,

but they can't count our kisses, kisses I'm
sure will stretch out beyond the end of time.

8.

You need to get that what is gone is lost.
Lying with her as each day's hot sun crossed
the sky, then you two were so deep in love.
Perhaps she started it; neither's above

the other once love's started. So much fun
you had together, and now it is done
and over. There is nothing you can do.
Whatever she wants now, it isn't you.

So tough it out, don't stalk her, be a mensch.
You will get over it. She won't. The wench
wrecked herself when she strutted off from you.
It was the end of love for her—it's true.

Scandal and age are hunting her with whips.
Who'll kiss you, bitch? Who'll nibble at your lips?

9.

Veranius, you are my closest friend—
you would be if I'd thirty thousand more
or if I added millions to the score.
I'm glad to hear you're at your journey's end,

your little household gods have welcomed you—
your brothers, your old mother. You are back.
And with you all your stories. You've a knack
for telling them, even when they're all true.

So, tell me how it was to visit Spain.
I am so very keen to see your face.
Tell me about each custom, tribe and place,
and snuggle up against my neck again

and kiss my eyes and lips. Of men who're blessed
I'll be much happier than all the rest.

10.

Young Varus and the girl who has his heart
walked with me at the Forum. She's some tart,
but polished, inoffensive. And our chat
was all about Bithynia and that,
mostly about whether I'd made a mint
out there. And so I had to say I'm skint.
It's a poor province; I did not get on
with my commander, nor did anyone.
He's just a fuckhead, hates all of his staff.
But Varus and his woman ignored half
of what I said. "You've clearly done quite well
for all you say you haven't. We can tell.
Eight sturdy bearers, that is not so bad."
I wanted to show off, although I'd had
no luck. I wanted to impress her, chose
to lie a bit. Looked round, and said, "Oh those.
I bought a job lot of eight men." I lied—
I didn't have a litter I could ride.
I didn't even have a broken chair
some slave could push. Nor anyone to wear
its struts around his neck. She caught me out.
"Catullus, dear," she said. "I'm here without
a litter. I would be so very pleased
if you'd lend yours. It is Serapis' feast
down at the temple." And I thought, oh no.
I damned her cheek, but said, "You have to go,
but those aren't mine, they're Cinna's. He's a friend
What's his is mine to use. But please do send

them back." I'd told a stupid fib in which
she'd caught me, made me blush. "You thoughtless bitch,"
I muttered—if I'd thought, I could have had
a lift back home. You've nabbed it first. Too bad.

11.

I know, boys, that you'd go to Timbuktu
for me. To the North Pole, the South one too.
You'd mingle with Jivaros who shrink heads
or with the gentle Japanese, whose beds

are hard if you're not used to them. You'd go
look at the Pyramids, eat Eskimo
cuisine, swim with piranhas, burn your feet
on Iceland's lava. If you want to treat

me right, you'll go and tell her, where she fucks
three hundred men queued up—the stupid schmucks,
she drains the juice from them and breaks their balls,
up that back alley with the come-smeared walls—

she snapped my heart off, like the flowers
some man drives over in your garden in his van.

12.

Asinius Marrucinus, your left hand
has sticky fingers. There is no excuse.
You weren't drunk. It's not funny. If you choose
to steal my table linen, you'll be banned

from all polite society. He's sad,
your brother Pollio. He'd gladly pay
for all your silly pranks to go away,
he's smart and witty, unlike you. We've had

enough of you. So kindly send it back
or get far ruder verses by return.
It was a present from my friends. You'll learn
value's not what things cost, but how their lack

hurts. It's not cloth alone they sent from Spain,
but love with it, until we kiss again.

13.

You'll dine well, Fabullus, round at my place
if it's convenient, in a few days.
Just bring some takeaway, perhaps Chinese
with rice and noodles. Chopsticks, if you please.

Also a pretty girl; it would be good
of you to bring some wine or beer. We could
play Cluedo, or Monopoly, or Chess,
if you could bring them round. There's wilderness

and winds and cobwebs in my wallet now
and little else. But I can tell you how
I will reward you, if you're kind. I've got
some perfume my girl brought me. Just a spot

will drive you wild. There's musk in it, and rose.
One whiff will make you pray to be all nose.

14.

Calvus, I didn't know you hated me.
Or why else send me such awful poetry?
I'd hate you back, but most assuredly
you'll have some reason, though I cannot see
what I have done to earn this penalty.
Own up, some client sent them as your fee—
Gods strike him with a pox or strangury—
and you thought that you'd share the misery.
Or is it some new and subtle tyranny
of Sulla's? Such an awful enemy
for you to have as client. Thankfully
at least that means he paid. I'd gladly flee
a room in that book's vague vicinity.
A gift that poisons eyes, quite mortally,
at Saturnalia too, a Upas tree
with candles. Next week, if my time is free
I'll fly round bookshops, buzzing like a bee
and bring you poisoned honey. One, two, three
big scrolls of rotten poets. Imagery
and metre that's a putrid mockery ...
and as for you, you little library
of awful stuff—off with you before we
set fire to you or sink you in the sea.
Go where you got those feet that limpingly
eke out your lines. Then stop.

15.

I'd trust you friend with every love of mine,
for you have standards. Some things you regard
as pure, untouchable. I know it's hard.
But do not touch that boy. He is so fine.

I am not worried random passers-by
will want to fuck him. Too much on their minds.
Your prick though, wanders. Into cute behinds,
often as not. I know you say you're bi,

can take or leave boys. So leave him alone,
make an exception, just for me. For it
is certain that I'll punish you, you shit,
if you betray me. Then you will atone

strung up to be abused by all who pass
with spiny fish and carrots up your arse.

16.

Eat out my pussy while I fuck you hard
my hands up both your arses. Silly boys,
you prissy queens, because my verse enjoys
making hot love, that doesn't mean I'm tarred

with the same filthy brush. I might be chaste
as anything. A poem might say "fuck,"
dabble its fingers in all kinds of muck,
turn people on perhaps, if they've a taste

for all that sort of thing. Old men with piles
don't get hard otherwise; bored wives are wet
reading my verses. But you still don't get
to think I'm slut or virgin. Snarky smiles

will get you hurt. Oh, I will make you shout,
fistfuck your arses while you eat me out.

17.

Colonna, little town, this is your chance.
You'd like a better bridge. This one's so small,
totters on shaky legs. One day will fall
if someone bounces on it. There's a dance
they call the cancan and they jump around.
Your citizens could do it up and down
a longer bridge. So funny. So, kind town.
I'd like a favour. Into the profound
and stinky mire it crosses, tip him in,
this ageing cuckold. Wanders round asleep,
a babe in arms. Down with him, fathoms deep
into the mud. His pretty wife is thin,
pecks like a sparrow my low hanging fruit,
she's young as spring and tender as a kid.
He wouldn't care whatever his wife did,
he doesn't ever notice just how cute
she is. Just lies there like King fucking Log.
I'd like just once to give the man a shake
and push him over so the fool would wake,
find himself stuck fast sinking in a bog
squelching around and desperate like a mule
in quicksand that pull off the iron shoe
each hoof in turn. That's what I'd have you do.
Town bridge marsh rid me of this blind deaf fool.

21.

Aurelius, the father of all lust,
all hunger, all desire there's ever been—
I know you well and what you want. I've seen
the way you look at him. I cannot trust

you around him, him around you. I know
you're after his sweet arse. You stand and joke
with him like you were friends, and share a smoke.
Before you fuck him, you will have to blow

me first. The thing that's getting up my nose
is, he is learning from you all your tricks,
your ways of getting what you want: hard dicks,
soft buttocks. He was nice once. I suppose

he'll change. It happens, but before you win,
my prick will fuck your mouth, and go right in.

22.

Suffenus has good manners, lots of charm,
and so prolific too. His books of verse
are beautifully printed; the reverse
of our small print run pamphlets. Where's the harm

in that? Nice typeface, every little stitch
in place, a nice production job thanks to
his publisher. But it's so sad when you
actually read his clumsy verses which

are witless, idiotic, countryfied,
verse with straw in its hair, a snotty nose.
But when he talks about it, you'd suppose
it great. He really would be mortified

if he knew what I think. To me this seems
a lesson in remembering motes and beams.

23.

Furius, your poor home lacks both safe and slave,
no hearth, too cold for spiders or for fleas.
Your father and your new stepmother have
teeth that can chew through flints as if through cheese.

And you're just snug there, for the three of you
get on so well. All of you have your health,
all of you look good. Nothing troubles you.
No arson, earthquakes, plots against your wealth,

no poisoners can harm you; danger stays
far off. Your bodies must have been freeze-dried
to be so tough. On Winter's coldest days
or when there's famine, father and his bride

and you are cheerful. And you still complain?
You never sweat or drool; your fine long nose
is never snotty. And you never deign
to fart or splatter shit. It's like a rose,

your sweet, intricate arse-hole, it's so clean
your friends could eat from it. And once a year
you squat ten minutes and produce a bean
or something like one, delicate and clear,

more like a pearl than shit. Your fingers touch
it and are not stained. Furius you're so
blessed in all ways so very very much
you do not need the tenner that I owe.

24.

Juventius, you're the cutest of the lot,
not just of your relations that exist
but those unborn. A fact you may have missed
about this new guy that you love—he's got

no money, none at all. The thing to do
with someone who's that poor is give him cash,
rather than think of giving him a screw.
He isn't good enough for you—so rash

of you to think he is—when he is broke,
no money and no servants to his name.
You're much too pretty, boy, to waste a poke
on someone shabby. It would be a shame

but you'll ignore me, do what you want, so
I'll mention that he's poor just so you know.

25.

Thallus, you ditzy queen, you're rabbit weak,
soft as a feather, cute as babies' ears.
When old men with soft dicks reach out and tweak
tired foreskins, you're more limp, but it appears

you have another side. Brisk like the wind
at dinner's end, when everyone is drunk
you grab stuff. Afterwards your host can't find
his favourite things—and they're all in your trunk.

My cashmere shawl, my Spanish linen and
my embossed stationery. They're all on show
in your apartment. I'd scratch on your hand
verses so rude that everyone would know

you steal—but you don't blush. Shame that would kill
most is for you just one more sexy thrill.

26.

The cottage you have outside town
is of all rustic dwellings the crown
O Furius you'll find
you don't need an ill wind
It's the mortgage will blow your house down.

27.

You've brought me wine that's dark and sweet,
so strong it tangles up my feet.
Sweet boy, I know I've had enough.
Bring me some paler, sharper stuff.

Postumia got some in. And she's the one
who gets to tell this party how much fun
to have and when to slacken off the pace.
Mind you, she's drunk herself. That cheerful face

is flushed from wine; her garland's all askew—
another drop of this, I'll be drunk too.
No, don't bring water. It just spoils the stuff
A waste of this good wine. I've had enough

Water's for older, sourer bitter men.
Perhaps I will toast Bacchus once again.

28.

You're off with Piso's legion, what a crew!,
your empty knapsacks ready for some loot.
My dear Veranus and Fabellus, shoot
the shit, what's up? I'm pretty sure that you

aren't any better off for all your toil,
bad food, worse drink. All your accounts will show
is on the debit side. How do I know?
My dear commander, Memmius, without oil

to smooth things, fucked me in the mouth and arse
for months, yet somehow it was me who laid
out cash without return. He never paid.
Piso's the same. Without a better class

Of boss, the gods will load you with disgrace,
You sorry dregs of the proud Roman race!

29.

How can we bear this? Only someone like
Mamurra could; he's shameless in his greed.
He's stripped the Gauls, the Britons too, and he'd
Make Romulus his bum boy. Like a pike

That strips a lake of fish, he leaves behind
Desolate emptiness. He seems so fair,
like an Adonis. And you took him there,
great Caesar, knowing your cute boy would find

so much to steal. Like pigeons, he will peck
until the garden's bare. He has devoured,
all his own cash, the loot of Spain. He scoured
the Black Sea coast sore. Now leaves Gaul a wreck,

Britain as well. What has he got on you?
Your marriage? Did he bugger that up too?

30.

Alfenus, you neglect and cheat your friends;
I needed help—you shunned me—I'd been good
to you, who have betrayed me. Heaven should
bring all fair-weather friends to sticky ends

And will. In what friends can men place their trust
when I have trusted you, who told me that
you were my loving friend? You dumped me flat
when I was wretched, who once said I must

rely on you above all else. You may
treat oaths as clouds the winds break up, erase
me from your mind and never leave a trace.
The gods remember broken trust. One day

Good Faith herself will rattle at your door
and it's with her you'll settle up the score.

31.

You shining jewel of islands, Sirmio,
and of peninsulas! Across the sea,
in other lands and lakes, there cannot be
a place that can compare at all. I'm so

glad to be safely back. I can't believe
Bithynia's behind me. You're a cure
for care and duties—I am very sure
the gods of hearth and home will soon relieve

my stress. To lie at home in my own bed
is what I've worked and dreamed and travelled for
these weary months. And there is nothing more,
a man could want. Now, tinkling in my head

I hear your wavelets lapping, laughing too.
Blessed place, blessed lake, blessed me for having you.

32.

Sweetest Ipsitilla, I'd really love
to come round after lunch, if that's OK,
You're sweet enough to be dessert. I'll say
such pretty things to you. So please remove

all other punters from your client book.
I really won't be happy if your door
is bolted when I get there. Please be sure
you don't go streetwalking that day. I'll look

for you. Stay in and do your nails and hair,
and dress up in your very nicest things.
I'll fuck you nine times. When your door-bell rings,
it will be me, so you'd better prepare

for shagging. Through my shirt and through my cloak,
you'll see my well-stuffed bloated pricklet poke.

33.

The biggest pests the baths have ever seen,
Vibennus is a thief. His son's a queen.
One's sticky fingers sneak into your bag,
the other's always asking for a shag.

Why don't you just fuck off and go to hell?
you with that hairy arse, which you can't sell
and you his thieving father. We all know
you steal, he sucks. Don't hang around. Just go.

34.

Pure boys and maidens
We sing to thee
Diana Queen of Chastity

Latona on fair Delos isle
rested under an olive tree
bore you and watched the infant smile
greatest of all Jove's progeny

Pure boys etc.

Mistress of every wooded peak
and of secluded forest glades
of swift high streams that foaming speak
and of the fields the forest shades

Pure boys etc.

Patron of women that give birth
and the reliever of their woe
queen of each crossroad on the earth,
as moon across the sky you go

Pure boys etc.

As moon you shed light on the soil
bringing the seasons round in turn
blessing the humble farmer's toil
bringing the harvest that he'll earn

Pure boys etc.

We worship you by every name
in every shape and aspect too
you have helped Rome; please be the same
to all of us who worship you

Pure boys etc.

35.

Go, letter, tell him now, the sensitive
poet Caecilius, that he should take
his leave from Como and its pretty lake
and hasten to Verona, where I live.

If he knew what I know, he would devour
the road in getting here, where I can share
the inner thoughts of one for whom we care,
although a pretty girl delays the hour

of his departure, throws her arms around
his neck, and begs him stay. The truth is though
it is his poem that set her aglow,
the one about Cybele. So profound

her lust to read the rest, I can't refuse
to think her, and not Sappho, the Tenth Muse.

36.

Volusius' histories, such awful shite,
I'll burn them and fulfil my Lesbia's vow
to Cupid and to Venus, that since now
our quarrel's over, poems I wrote in spite

against her should be burned. Here's what she said:
"The worst poets' finest verses to the flames
of lame old Vulcan." She invoked your names
and laughed. Sweet malice gets into her head

sometimes. So here's the deal, you shining pair,
you who rose from the foam, and you, blind boy
whose arrows hurt us—please may I employ
a stratagem? I think that this is fair—

I'll burn instead of my works full of wit,
Volusius' stuff—which is authentic shit.

37.

Such a foul bar, with fouler clientele,
to be so near the Twin's shrine! All you dicks
who think you are the only one with pricks
that no-one else could ever fuck as well

the women who hang out there. I will make
all of you suck my cock. I'll advertise
what your pub's for. I'll draw dicks of huge size
upon your sign. My wounded heart will break

because she's there and fucks the lot of you,
the girl I love. She takes you all out back
into the alley, and she has no lack
of men who'll wait to fuck her, in a queue.

She's fondest of Ignatius by a mile—
his scruffy beard, his stinking piss-washed smile

38.

Cornificius, I'm so very sad.
Oh god, I'm sad, and it is getting worse
each hour, each day. And you are really bad
at kissing it all better. The reverse

is true. I'm pissed that you can't soothe
my pain with comfort. I am sadder than
Simonides, the poet of doleful truth,
who tried and failed to find an honest man.

39.

You grin too much; we know your teeth shine white.
Some thug's life's being begged for by his brief
some mother's burying her son—such grief!—
you're there and so's the smile. It's not polite

Egnatius; people think you've some disease—
paralysis or madness. It's poor style
and out of fashion. This inane fixed smile
makes me quite ill. I wish you'd shut it, please.

Sabines, Etruscans, Umbrians and such
use running water when they clean their teeth.
Same with us in Verona. It's beneath
our dignity to smile so very much.

Worse, you're from Spain, and the real trouble is
we know you wash your gums and teeth with piss.

40.

Poor little Ravidus, just what's possessed
you to dive headlong in my verses' way?
Perhaps some spiteful god chose to suggest
that you should come here and start a melee

or maybe you want fame. That's why you shove
your nose in here. My verse is hard enough
to punish those who trespass on my love
with years and years of angry bitter stuff.

41.

That shagged out tart Amaena—what a nerve!—
has dunned me for a grand. I don't deserve
this shit from bankrupt Formianus' screw,
her friends know she's not well, her doctors too.

She has a nose so twisted it's obscene;
you are her family, please intervene.
She flinches when she sees a looking glass.
I'd never pay to fuck her scraggy arse.

42.

Fuck, felch, quim, rim—I need you at my side,
you dirty little words. She thinks it's smart
to pad her tits with verse, to take my art
and wipe her arse. And I've already tried

to ask her nicely; she is now fair game.
So, hang around her shag pad's open doors;
you'll know her instantly. The other whores
pull faces and their skirts aside. Her name

is filthy just like you. So cluster round,
jostle her, pinch her, mug her, shout out loud,
"Give him his poems back." And in a crowd
say she's the long-lost mother that you've found.

And if that doesn't work, then simply try
to ask her nicely, beg, or even cry.

43.

You haven't an especially small nose;
your feet don't have high arches and cute toes.
Your eyes don't flash like wildfire in the night;
your fingers are quite stubby, and the nails
bitten and badly painted—those are fails.
You drool a bit; you're really not so bright
And you've an Tuscan accent; I can see
you're some little provincial nobody
who's dating someone from your neighbourhood
who's rich enough buy you clothes; he could
buy smarter. You will do, but not in Rome;
go be a famous beauty near your home.
Lesbia dates me; you're not in her class.
Degenerate age, to think you almost pass.

44.

Only my friends think that my villa's chic.
Suburbs have borders and it straddles one
where posh meets not quite classy. I have fun
there anyway; and loved the place last week

when I'd an awful cough, a stomach flu
I'd been out dining and perhaps the food
or wine upset me. Or perhaps it could
have been—since the wrong book can poison you—

that I read Sestianus' speech. It's rough
against his enemies. My chest gets tight.
I choke and cough and puke half of the night
when I go there, and have to read his stuff.

I'd rather get my health back here at home
than be made ill by prose and wine in Rome.

45.

Septimus held his love Acme and said,
"May I be struck down if I should ever fail
to love you madly? May I rot in jail,
get eaten by a lion or drop down dead!"

Cupid sneezed twice in blessing. Acme kissed
her sweet boy's eyes. "My limbs and organs burn
with gorgeous fire. So let us love, and earn
the gifts of our true master. Let him list

us with the truest lovers he has blessed."
The god sneezed twice more. No-one's ever been
happier than these two or has ever seen
love quite so much more true than all the rest.

Offer them wealth, or provinces to rule,
instead of love—they'd smile and call you fool.

46.

Now spring will drive harsh winter's cold away;
and howling gales shrink to a gentle breeze.
In Phrygia you either burn or freeze,
so take your leave, Catullus, go and play

in Asia's cities. It's the time of year
when we're all on the move. So friends, let's go
our separate ways. We'll meet again, I know,
once we get home, just as we met out here.

47.

Piso would rather have you round to dine—
his foul left hands who wipe his scabby arse—
than do the decent thing by friends of mine.
The god of pricks, he really has no class.

Socration and Porcius, you pair,
he wines you, dines you, gives you every treat.
Fabellus and Veranus live on air
and beg for invitations in the street.

48.

Juventius, to kiss your eyes is sweet,
as honey. I will not be satisfied
with thirty million kisses—so complete
is my devotion, I've not even tried
to cease from kissing. In a field of wheat,
harvest the grain and put each grain beside
the kisses I will give you. We'll defeat
comparison, then kiss once more in pride.

49.

Most golden-tongued of Romans, Cicero,
the greatest advocate we'll ever know,
I'm forced to offer you my thanks, although
you hate my verse. And if it ranks below
your work in worth, that's really not so bad,
since you're the greatest writer that we've had.

50.

We were up late. Our keyboards nearly burned
from all the jokes and bitching, even verse.
My head hurt. It's as if I somehow earned
pain you'd expect from wine from wit. The worse

I feel, the better time I know I had—
I wanted more. Why can't it be the same
when we're together? Would it be so bad?
Why is our conversation always tame

the nights we're fucking? Lying in your bed,
legs wrapped around each other, pretty boy,
this simple verse is beating in my head.
We mustn't want too much. It might annoy

the goddess Nemesis. That horrid bitch.
She keeps us poor in love, who could be rich.

51.

He's like a god, I think, or maybe more
than gods, the man who's sitting next to you,
he gets to watch you. It is almost too
much that he hears your sweet laugh. I am poor

in spirit, Lesbia, because that sound
robs me of sense. It leaves me blind and dumb.
Soon deafness and paralysis will come.
I moan, and stagger, lie there on the ground,

and that's just when you laugh. I cannot bear
to think of him, or you. And worse by far,
I know the truth, that all my problems are
trivial, and silly, lighter than the air

and yet great kingdoms fall through such as this,
an idle dreamer, longing for a kiss.

52.

Come on, Catullus, die. You might as well.
That pustule Nonius sits as a judge
Vatinius is consul by some fudge
And broken oaths. So die, you might as well.

53.

I had to laugh, when some guy in the crowd
amazed at how dear Calvus talked us through
Vatinius' crimes so clearly, said aloud,
"This man's so miniscule and speaks well too."

54.

Otho shits down his legs. You cannot take
him anywhere. His head is tiny too.
Libo has gentle farts. You could mistake
them for a sigh or breeze. I hope that you
are getting irritated, Caesar. I could make
fun of Sufficius, next—somehow it's true
he's senile yet again. Great Lord, I'll make
fun of your friends to make fun of you too.

55.

You know, if it's not too much of a bore
we'd like to know where you hang out these days.
Looked on the Heath, and round the Dilly. More,
checked Foyles, St Pauls, even Hampton Court Maze.

You're nowhere. Checked the girls up at King's Cross:
they hadn't seen you. One pulled out her tits,
said, "He's in here." You may not give a toss
but having all these girls show us their bits,

not our idea of fun. A full time job.
So, ring us, e-mail us, and make a date
to dish the dirt. Or, if you like, your gob
stays shut and schtum. Call us at any rate

We've gossip of our own we'd like to share.
Not telling you it burns. It's just not fair.

56.

Oh Cato, you'll laugh when you hear.
So lend me your mouth and your ear.
I caught a boy fucking
some girl, so I snuck in
and buggered him, stiff as a spear.

57.

It's turned out nice again for that sweet pair,
Caesar and his Mamurrus. You might stare
in wonder, but it's really no surprise.
They're just alike—one has the other's eyes—

although one's Roman, one from Formiae.
They've oozed over each other like a dye
they never will wash off, or a disease
that they're both sick with. They are twins in sleaze

who've taught each other cunning tricks in bed.
They share all things, and give each other head,
and they swap wives, especially their own,
and hand their fucks over without a groan

except for little girls'. You know it's true.
They've fucked each other and they'll fuck Rome too.

58.

Oh Caelius, Caelius, what's this I hear?
That Lesbia who was to us so dear,
the woman I, Catullus, held above
myself, my name and everything I love
she stands around on sordid Roman streets—
giving hand-jobs to every dick she meets.

58b.

I'd need to have the feet Daedalus made
for his vast robot, Talos, who could run
round Crete thrice every day, or chase the sun
on Pegasus or have the boots inlaid

with wings on which the hero Perseus flew
or Rhesus' snow-white chariot-racing team.
I'd have to fly the way I do in dream.
Winged feet. Winged horses. And my own wings too.

If you could give me those—you move so fast
that you must have them. No-one ever finds
you. You must have the speed of winds
to hide from all your friends. And then, at last,

when I catch up to you, tired to the bone
from chasing, I'd fall down, sleep like a stone.

59.

There's this redhead in Bologna likes to blow
any random redhaired fellow you might know.
She is married to Menenus. She will go
round the graveyard, seeking dinner, to and fro,
grabbing bread out of the embers where they glow
of cremations. And the sexton hates her so,
he won't shave until he kills her with one blow.

60.

A lioness more deadly than its male
who roams the desert seeking to devour
all that it can. Its eyes have evil power
to paralyze. The lashing of its tail

is terrible. Imprisoned on her isle
Scylla has tentacles, dogs at her waist.
Six snake-heads her own human face replaced.
She was once beautiful, known for her smile

No longer. From some monster you were born,
one such as these. You clawed your vicious way
out of their womb, and afterwards they lay
dead, torn and bleeding. That is why such scorn

is in your heart for one who'll simply kneel
and beg for love from you, who does not feel.

61.

Hymen, lord of weddings come,
from Helicon, your mountain home.
Urania, star-gazing muse,
taught you her son which days to choose
to bring the bridegroom his sweet bride.
Hymen!

Come to us. Wreathed around your head
bright flowers and a veil that's red,
scented with marjoram that's sweet,
and on your delicate white feet
your orange sandals neatly tied.
Hymen!

Wake on this day without a care.
Toss flaming torches through the air,
shake the ground with stamping dance!
Sing falsetto wedding chants.
Julia weds Manlius!
Hymen!

She comes to him, and is as fair
as Venus was. Wrapped in her hair
and little else, to face the choice
that Paris made. So now rejoice
she is the prettiest of us.
Hymen!

Sweet scented as the myrtle tree
when all its twigs have flowers is she.
The wood-nymphs sprinkle every one
with dew. Transluscent droplets run,
are worn like pearls by every flower.
Hymen!

Come from the chilling mountain pools
where the nymph Aganippe cools
Aonia's caves, each drip a shock
that trickles down from rock to rock
still freezing cold after an hour.
Hymen!

Summon the bride to her new home
and her new man. They'll never roam,
with love entwine them. Slowly bind
each heart to heart and mind to mind
as growing ivy shrouds a tree.
Hymen!

And you, young virgins, sing along
this cheerful little wedding song.
This is her day, your day comes soon,
so celebrate her honeymoon.
He's her friend now, yours soon he'll be.
Hymen!

He hears us call him when we sing
his praise. It is such praise will bring
him cheerfully, the god who'll lead
Venus behind him. Love will need
his help so lovers call his aid.
Hymen!

What other god could they ask more
but Hymen? Or whose help implore?
We worship you because we seek
your help. Without you love is weak;
it is Hymen that makes it strong.
Hymen!

And frightened parents ask your aid.
Safeguard their daughters. They're afraid
as they undress for their new man.
You help each girl, show her she can
be naked and still have no shame.
Hymen!

You hold their innocence in trust,
ensure that love is not just lust.
Each girl can give herself away
just as her mother did one day
because they do it in your name.
Hymen!

Without you there's no good in love.
Without you, love will soon remove
good name. And you make it all right
to make love on a wedding night.
No other god can quite compare.
Hymen!

Without your help, fathers can't know
a child is theirs. It's you that show
each child is where it ought to be.
Your rites bring lands stability
that no god else can ever share.
Hymen!

Now Junia's at the bedroom door
And it is open. Up they soar—
the torch flames gleam like locks of hair.
Shame makes her stand and weep but there
is no more time. She has to go.
Hymen!

Junia, you need not cry, for none
more beautiful has seen the sun
rise from the sea, bring the new day.
You need not fear—there is no way
you'll bring disgrace upon your clan.
Hymen!

Fair as a many coloured flower,
a hyacinth in some small bower,
a rich man's place where fountains play.
It is the time. No more delay,
he's waiting for you, your sweet man.
Hymen!

No more delay. It is the time.
Now listen to us, to our rhyme,
each torch now turns its face away.
It's over now, your wedding day
and now begins your wedding night.
Hymen!

Don't be afraid. He'll be your friend,
this night will seem without an end.
The pain is short, pleasure will last.
So long it seems like days have passed,
when darkness leads to early light.
Hymen!

He'll be a good man, not a rake.
He'll never cheat, or ever take
some slut as mistress, be a joke
or scandal, as do many folk.
At home he'll nuzzle at your breasts.
Hymen!

As some sweet smelling clinging vine
around a tree will slow entwine,
catch him up in a sweet caress
this moment. You will always bless
this time when his head on you rests.
Hymen!

And on this night that you are wed
the ivory-footed wedding bed
is where it all begins, the joys
that marriage sensually deploys
to bind each woman to her man.
Hymen!

So raise the torches high above
the flaming symbols of the love
that Hymen seals between this pair.
Now raise the torches in the air
as has been done since time began.
Hymen!

Now silence all the bawdy song,
the smooth-faced eunuchs sing along
and give the boys their tasty treat,
shelled walnuts with the sweetest meat
as they say farewell to the groom.
Hymen!

He never shagged a country maid—
it was his hairdresser he laid.
But husbands quit that kind of thing
the moment they put on the ring
and join their sweet bride in her room.
Hymen!

The nervous bride has found her place
not just in her husband's embrace.
This is the house where she'll grow old,
she'll be white-haired but never cold,
she will be taken good care of.
Hymen!

She'll show her elegant small feet
to him who'll find them tender sweet
to kiss in foreplay. Then he'll take
his time with her and slowly make
his actions symbols of their love.
Hymen!

Her aunts will dress her; maidens lead
her to her bed; she will not need
their help for long. Her heart's a flame
but quietly for she has shame.
They leave her, leave the door ajar.
Hymen!

Now husband come—your bride is fair.
She's dressed and has undone her hair
Her lips are bright and poppy-red,
her skin is white against the bed
as daisies or as lilies are.
Hymen!

And, husband, just get on with it.
You're gorgeous too, you'll be a hit,
Venus will help—she fancies you
and if she does, your wife will too,
so hot she'll set the bed on fire.
Hymen!

Make love at once and don't delay,
Venus will help you in your play.
She likes it when you really can't
try to conceal the things you want
and are just dizzy with desire.
Hymen!

The one who wants to count the ways
you'll make sweet love in these first days
in Africa should count the sand
or reckon stars. You'll have in hand
the time for so much venery.
Hymen!

Play as you like, but keep in mind
children should not be far behind.
An old house needs its new recruits
and small buds spring from ancient roots.
Weddings must lead to progeny.
Hymen!

Tiny Torquatus will reach out
his tiny hand. Father will shout
how like they are except in size
and that he has his mother's eyes.
Neither has any guilt nor shame.
Hymen

When babies look just like their dad
it means their mother's not been bad.
And everyone can know it's true
just what is what and who is who,
and who's entitled to a name.
Hymen!

The first-born shows the quality
of parents and their family.
Penelope gets her good name
her measure of immortal fame
from how Telemachus was born.
Hymen!

It's time you maidens shut the door.
We've seen enough, we don't need more.
You two, this is your wedding night,
do what you have to, do it right!
The night is short. Soon comes the dawn.
Hymen!

62.

The evening star is up. Together boys.
Put down your glasses. Leave half-eaten plates.
This is the moment marriage celebrates
the moment that fulfils.

But it destroys.
We dread that star ... but now the boys excel.
Step forward singing thrusting in their dance
so very fine, of course, this is our chance
to show them up and have our fun as well.

The girls have practiced, that is what girls do.
They concentrate. Other things on our minds.
Booze games. Yet when a young man's ego finds
girls doing better, he and his whole crew
get louder, faster put girls in their place.

Cities are sacked. Terrible things are done.
Worse this, our friend is given to someone,
some boy steps up, tears her from the embrace
of friends and mother.

Evening star, your flame
brings families together, it unites
men who would otherwise in pointless fights
wreck cities. Let us praise your saviour name.

She's stolen.

Yes, no matter how the guards
stay up all night with lanterns, comes the day
the rising star of marriage steals away
your friend, and her white dress, old name discards.

Rare, delicate, a flower under glass
is watered, safe from random cows. No plough
uproots it. But once picked it withers now
or someone tears off petals. When we pass
from virgin into wife we cut all ties.
Plucked from us, our companions. All delight
the girls, the young men, had at every sight
of our chaste beauty like cut flower dies.

Vine by itself a creeper on the ground
whose tendrils' shallow purchase takes no root,
never produces mellow swelling fruit
but if it's fortunate it will have found
stout elm or oak to bind to. Or a stake:
the vineyard owner lifts it, cultivates,
trims it and waters. Fertilises. Waits.
Grapes weigh down, bend stake, tree, which never breaks.

Together sing. Your maidenhead's a knot,
untied it is a contract. Roman law
says that it is your flesh but something more,
your father's oath, all honour he has got,
your mother's care. When you were born her pain.
We end. Sing Hymen's wedding worship praise!
This night the start of all your future days.
Hymen! Boys girls unite in this refrain!

63.

Attis hurries. Runs barefoot,
takes a fast boat to Asia,
runs again.
Mad with Her love so that he feels no pain.
He loves.
Comes to Her woods and groves.
Then starts to cut
cut with the flint that cut
feet.
Cuts deep and fast.
The blood begins to flow.
She plucks the last
bits of her former flesh
out by the chords
No.
Takes off their weight
loses that weight.
So
And slash
No words for what she feels
new made at her own hand
blood gushes on the trampled earth
at this new birth
of who she is,
of what he was,
of who she will be,
what he cannot be.
Her hand

suddenly delicate white hand
seizes the tambourine
the little tintinabulinking
tambourine
the drums, the drums as white, the calfskin drums,
drums of Her sacrifice
cut from the bull-calf.
Stretched
stretched
drum beaten by the white hand
the light hand
fierce.
She sings soprano, sopranino, mezzo mezzo to the band
of her new friends, her sisters of the cut
who beat the drums
and wave the tambourines
and dance upon the ground the bloody ground
the sound, the echo sound, the piercing sound
of Goddess rite.

Step forward, step back, one two three,
left, forward, right, back, one two three,
stamp skip step, stamp skip step,
stamp skip and kick.
Step, stamp and kick.
We are the girls, kick,
girls of the cut, step,
cows for our Lady, stamp.
To her woods we go, step.
Far far from home, kick,
exiles for ever, left,

birds of a feather, back.
Sisters of cutting, kick.
Follow my lead, stamp.
Cast aside Love, kick,
watch Goddess laugh, left.
Hurry together, kick.
Dance to her house, right,
deep in the woods, stamp.

Where there are flutes, kick,
where Maenads shake it, back,
wild curly locks, left.
Cymbals clash, crancrancrancran
drums beat, ratatata
Howl howl howl howl
Honour the goddess,
one two and three, stamp,
one two and three, kick.

Attis dances, Attis sings.
Attis new girled.
Howls. Howls. Ulualalalu
Drum ratata, cymbal ratat.
Up to the mountains
wild in the trance.
Out of breath out of mind fast stamping chorus
bleeding bleeding white
Drum ratatat
Cows moomoo ullalalu new
to the yoke
the goddess' yoke.

The goddess house.
Where they drop
drop
sleep
starved
emptied
and frenzy
done.

Glare of the morning. Sky burned clear.
Waking sun.
Line of light across the harsh rocks,
the dry land, the scrub land, the merciless sea.
Wild horses of the sun
chase shadows of the night.
And Attis
wakes.
Wakes in the arms
of the mother goddess of all gods.
Calm of frenzy
Awake
Fresh from cutting, fresh from dancing,
voice clear.
Looks out across the sea
and sings homesick regret.
Aria.
O patria mea
quanto mi costa
Distress
you made me you undo me
mother and mistress,

I flee you
as slaves flee.
Up to the high hills
the hills are so cold
the wild beasts shiver
among them am I
snuggling in dens.
Oh country,
mother and mistress.
Are you here, am I there?
You have high hills
where trees shake in winds.
This is my home
driven by frenzy
far from good people kind people gentle folk
High harsh hills.
I am not in the forum and I am not in the gym
I am not in the market place or running round the track
I am no more that person and will never more be him
I've left my home forever and I'm never coming back
Regret regret regret. Ullalulalu
What does she look like
what do I?
Woman—stamp
Boy—stamp
Husband—stamp
groom—stamp
girlfriend—stamp.
Wife—stamp
Eunuch—stamp.
Maenad—stampstampstamp.

I was so cool
they loved me in school
the best in the gym,
they asked me to tea,
they turned on the fans,
they brought me flowers, so many flowers.
And that's all gone, ullalalu
up in the high hills.
Cut.
Like a slave
slave to the goddess.
Wild hair, and bleeding, cut.
Ullalalu
Among the pines
with boars and deer.
What have I done?
Ullalalu.
Mercy, mother, mercy. Hear my woe, ullalalu

The goddess heard.
Her lions roared
the long-maned lions who pull her chariot,
sweet chariot.
And said.
ROAR
ROAR
Drive Her Mad
With your Roar.
Whip her to frenzy with your lashing tails
that lash, that smash, that slash.
ROAR
let her feel claw.

So she's mad. Mad.
Then let her run mad fingers through your mane
your hair your lovely hair
your strong neck.

Goddess takes the yoke from off their necks
The lions howl, and prowl and yowl
There is a crackle in the undergrowth
it's lions seeking prey, tracking prey,
prey that runs from the hill
crosses the stream.
Running water running water
Make me safe.
Tracking Attis as she prays
kneels in the sand
looks across the sea.
White sand under delicate white knees.
And
They
Pounce,
Roar
In her Ear.
Drive her quite mad
Slave forever. Slave to the goddess.

Goddess, hear my plea
Goddess, stay away
Her but not me.
Attis but not me.
Ullalalu
Cut

64.

Tall pines that grew on mountains now afloat,
they coast and then they enter the Black Sea
heading for Colchis. Somehow they agree,
all of Earth's Mightiest Heroes on a boat,
a single purpose: take the Golden Fleece.
The ship skims fast, an arrow from a bow,
across the waves. Heart pulse strokes heroes row
draw back a moment's pause sight then release.
Athena clever laid the ribs and keel
of this first ship. Goddess of the high place
whose shield's enameled with the Gorgon's face,
who gives us all she knows—no need to steal—
and as the Argo fought its way through foam
its oars kicked up on waves, they rose and gazed.
At this new spectacle they were amazed,
the gorgeous nymphs who make the sea their home
stared at the heroes who stared back in lust,
large-breasted naked women who appear
from nowhere. The heroes ship their oars and leer.
Heroes are men who will do what men must.
Peleus though saw her and lost his heart
and Thetis caught his glance and lost hers too,
though he was mortal. Knew that, as men do,
he'd die and leave. And hers the sadder part.
Her father blessed the match, Nereus the good,
lord of calm seas. Oh, heroes hail!
Courage and virtue! Strength that would prevail
against all odds! I really wish I could

do justice in my verse. To mothers born
whose virtues made gods love them and then woo.
And Peleus most of all I will praise you,
Thessaly's Lord, whose wealth is cows and corn.
Gods and men praise you. Jupiter will lead
the bride he wooed until a prophesy
told him her son would always greater be
than any father. Jupiter must cede
her to a mortal love. Her sisters there,
the Nereids. All seagods celebrate
Tethys deep mother Oceanus the great.
Coral and seashells decorate her hair.
Nor gods alone: from Scyros' rock-strewn shore
and from Pharsalia the peasants throng.
And all of Thessaly unites in song
to hymn this wedding. The yoked oxen snore—
there's none to drive them—soil forgets the plough,
which rusts abandoned; trees remain unpolled,
and vines untrimmed. The smithy's fire grows cold,
dust on the hammers. See the palace now
glistens with gold and silver. Ivory of Hind
frames every couch, purple with Tyrian dye
the cushions. Everything delights the eye.
Bedchamber fit for goddess where she'll find
not only luxury, instruction too.
Improving stories decorate each wall,
how heroes faced adversity and all
triumphed at last. But there is sadness too:
the counterpane embroidered shows the tale.
Abandoned Ariadne wakes from sleep.
Perhaps he drugged her. Her confusion's deep.

His ship is gone and she begins to wail,
seeing it in the distance out at sea.
She stares wild-eyed dishevelled in her grief.
The youth she loved, worse than any thief,
with broken vows took her virginity,
left fast as wind. The combs that pinned her hair
with pebbles at her feet. And her torn dress,
rags washed up by the surf. In her distress
tears saltier than the breakers, cries drown out
the sound of pounding waves and seabirds' scream.
And in her mind a thousand sorrows teem.
Love tortures her with pangs as sharp as thorns,
has ever since that boy from Athens came
to Crete to win his glory out of shame,
the slaughter of her eldest brother, born
all-winning Androgeos, envy slew.
Athenian athletes could not stand to lose
the games. Crete's not the enemy to choose.
Defeat you first then call down plague on you.
King Minos had two problems—one more son,
ravenous bullhead raging Minotaur,
and to ensure that never in fierce war
could Athens rise and menace anyone,
stripped of its fairest maids and best young men
butchered and eaten down to guts and bones.
That is the way that Athens now atones,
Minos ensures it will not rise again.
But duty called him from his hidden place,
the secret hero Prince who now set sail.
He'd heard Athenian father's, mother's wail,
and came to Knossos. When she saw his face

she rose a virgin girl from where she lay,
safe, clean, in mother's arms. As myrtle flowers
unfold sweet smelling stars, as late spring showers
unfurl the daffodils, as focused ray
will catch dry grass and set it all on fire,
so blooms so fires her body with desire.
She falls in love and cannot look away.
Savage boy archer who undoes us all
with arrows tipped with anguish and with joy,
and mother crueller than the rosewinged boy
how hard you made poor Ariadne fall
for Theseus, how often made her faint
with grief, for she would save him if she could,
victorious or else her brother's food,
her face as white as if Columbine's paint
were daubed on it. And so she swore her vow
in silence with lips tight and solemnly,
before approving gods, who always see
love that is true. But see her hero now!
Oaks pulled out root by root in hurricane
or pines a storm has taken snapped like sticks.
So lies her brother. And one last hoof kicks
and then is still. Great eyes grow dull with pain
and then with death. Lies a colossal wreck.
Theseus seized him by his mighty horns
wrenched them apart just like a wrestler born
then twisted. Smashed his skull and broke his neck.
Lost in the dark and caught in tortuous ways,
he and the other hostages are starved and dead
had she not given him the golden thread.
No other way from craftsman Daedalus' maze.

So little left to tell. They fled away.
Her father's wrath, her mother's loving tears,
her sister's kindness. None of this appears
to matter to her. Minos, Pasiphae
and Phaedra she forgets. And now, today,
she pays the price. Abandoned on the shore
the husband she preferred to all her kin
brought her to Naxos, stripped her to the skin,
took pleasure. She to him meant nothing more,
and so he sailed away. Her heart aflame
with shame and disappointment hear her cry
salt tears into the sea until, eyes dry,
she climbs the high cliffs and she shrieks his name,
looks at vast empty sea which does not care,
seethes heaves regardless of her. She is all alone,
half-naked. Cold waves chill her to the bone,
sun burns her. And as she is standing there,
this her lament. "You are the worst of men,
Prince Theseus. You left me here to die
on this bare shore. Each promise was a lie.
Before the gods you swore and swore again.
There's consequences for your perjuries,
although you seem to think quite otherwise,
and think to sail back home with all your lies
floating behind you scattered to the breeze.
Merciless, faithless, pitiless and cruel,
you talked of marriage. But the only bed
you led me to, this beach. I lie unwed,
dishonoured and abandoned and a fool.
Women beware of men who drunk on lust,
will promise anything to get their way,

but once they've had you saunter on their way.
Lust spent and whistling. Leave you in the dust.
Without me you'd be dead and torn apart.
I chose you, not my brother, poor dumb beast,
you'd think you'd have some gratitude at least.
Some qualm or some compassion in his heart.
Vultures or gulls will peck my corpse quite clean.
The surf will wear my bones down into sand.
No rite no tomb no final helping hand
to place coins on my eyes. You must have been
ripped from some lioness, or savage sea
spat you from storm, or maelstrom. Scylla foul
licked you with many tongues free of your caul,
not born, created to bring misery.
Or unloved let me serve you as your maid,
a basin of cold water for your feet,
or on your bed I'd lay a fresh ironed sheet,
neat corners. I am utterly betrayed.
There's none to hear me but the howling wind,
which does not understand and does not care,
and will not answer me and will not share
my sadness as a friend, I'm left behind,
no-one will come here, he will not return.
How did I earn your scorn, Fate? You don't hear
my pleas, or judge them with a hostile ear.
Jupiter turn back time. He never came
to Knossos hostage, never used his charm
to win me, never brought my brother harm.
I never saw him. Never heard his name.
All comfort and all refuge are denied
to me. I do not know how I might seek

to cross the seas and find some Cretan peak
and die upon a barren mountainside
which would be home at least. My father's face
is turned from mine, smeared with my brother's blood.
My loving husband means me nothing good,
sails far from vows he swore. And in this place
there is no shelter, just an empty shore
and rocks. No hope that I can find a way
to live or leave. Sky, sea and land are gray,
despair, death, desolation. Nothing more.
Yet, gods, before I'm silent, before death
darkens my sight and takes my sense away,
listen to these last words I'll ever say,
with rage and sorrow choking my last breath,
gods punish my betrayer. Furies come,
you Kindly Ones, women with snakes for hair,
and listen to my curse complaint and prayer.
May vengeance right and tidy as a sum
requite just anger burning in my veins
like fire and frenzy bonecrack mad and wild
abandoned wife, lost love and disowned child,
for every pain I feel may equal pains
afflict him. May the consequence of sin
be this. Through his own fault may he destroy
those he loves most. May that forgetful boy
through carelessness become death to his kin!
Megaera's withering glance, Allecto's whip,
Tisiphone's infecting ragged nails,
goddesses of revenge that never fails.
I breathe out wrath. Come, cast it at his ship!"
Her grief, her sighs were answered by a Nod

that split the waters, made the mountains shake.
The glittering bowl of stars seemed like to break.
Sad angry words had touched the heart of God.
And so it was. As Theseus neared the coast
his mind was clouded. He forgot them quite
and did not change the sails as black as night
his ship bore. Told by him he loved the most,
his father, who had told him when he left
Athens for Crete, just how, at his return,
he might reduce suspense. For old men burn
like boys with expectation. "I bereft,
so soon of my late found and unknown son,
new father with white hair must let you go
to do what heroes do. Of course I know
we have no better choice. For what was done
to Crete's dead prince we've had to pay the price.
If there's a chance to end our punishment
we need to try—Minos will not relent—
for better fortune we must throw the dice.
Yet I'm allowed to fear and to complain,
stare at you, tears in eyes, and hug you close.
A father sends his son to war. He knows
it's in the hands of gods whether again
they'll see each other. Oh, Athena, maid
and warrior, upon my head I pour
ashes in grief. He fights the Minotaur.
Help him to win. My son, see I have made
sable black sails as tokens of my grief.
Let winds of sorrow bear you on your way
but if you should come back, upon that day,
change them for white. My sadness or relief

are in your hands. Be mindful of both sails.
Do not forget.' Her curse strikes and he fails.
His father on the highest roof of town
waits weeping hoping. Then he catches sight
of Theseus' ship with sails as black as night
and in despair the old man tumbles down
despairing or distracted. And his blood
flows slowly to the water's edge to greet
his son who finds it lapping at his feet,
and then remembers late the sails he should
have changed. And then is tortured in his mind
with dark regret that drives him almost mad,
knows grief equivalent to what he had
inflicted on the wife he left behind.
And elsewhere on the tapestry was shown
the happy ending that would come at last
for Ariadne. She'd forget her past
in wine-flushed Bacchus' arms. In bright thread sewn
his troupe Bachantes, Silenus old sot
dancing and staggering a tipsy line,
wandering in all directions. Tipped with pine
cones are the staves that some of them have got
and wave around; others fresh slaughtered deer
are waving, bloody joint, liver and gut
others fall to the ground in dog piles rut.
(There's many a peeping Tom would love it here).
Some kiss snake lips and wreathe them round each limb
or clash brass cymbals. Oh the steady beat
anachronistic tap shod dancing feet.
Obscene and raucous is their coarse wild hymn,
they blow brass trumpets, hit their tambourines,

and skirling bagpipes in a steady drone,
bassoons and serpents in a steady moan,
they cry Evoe. I don't know what that means.
They walk around the palace, see each sight
and then the populace begin to drift
away. They know they're only the first shift
of guests. You know, how at the end of night
the twilit West Wind blows upon the sea,
starts little waves at first but with the dawn
middling billows, breakers great are born
that rush to shore and roar. First quietly
then in a rush Thessalians depart.
They know social encounters with a god
can end quite badly. If you're in a crowd
and someone curses very very loud
don't try to find out on whose foot you trod.
Chiron the centaur came first. He who taught
heroes then heroes' sons. The flowers of spring,
the fruits of summer, autumn harvest, bring
to this great feast! All in one basket caught
to great delight. River god Peneus,
besides whose waters groves and forests grow,
brought all the sheltering green trees that we know
willow and laurel, cedar and ficus,
poplar and plane, all tall and smelling sweet
it's now full noon. The wedding needs such trees
on a bright day with very little breeze
protect the guests and servers from the heat.
Prometheus whose wounds are hardly scars
where eagle ate his liver, where he hung
chained to a Scythian mountain as was sung

by poets. Then all crowned with brightest stars
the father of the gods, his wife, their kin—
save Phoebus and Diana who disdain
the loss of maidenhood—and their train.
Let every god who's present eat! Begin!
Old women in white garments then appear,
their bodies tremble but their hands don't shake.
They spin out threads—beware if yours should break—
no god has ever seen them without fear.
They know of every life and every death,
how short how soon, these sisters are the Fates.
Weave tapestries that tell us all our dates,
a baby's bottom's slapped to give her breath
and finally two coins will close her eyes,
they see it all at once and no surprise
will ever touch them birth then life then death,
these wise old bitches come. Glare and advance,
left hand on spindle. Fresh sheared fresh washed wool,
a ragged mess that into lives they pull
and bite tie off each thread. A constant dance
stills conversation. And their eyes are dim,
drip tears, but it's from too much truth, not age,
their oracles better than any sage
can tell from stars or cards. But always grim.
And this their wedding chant with its refrain
"We spin. We weave. We cut." A constant bass,
and soon there's agony on every face,
and too much knowledge beating in each brain,
softly at first and kindly. "Bride and groom,
always in love, forever, that is true,
and no misfortune ever comes to you.

Save this, you know your son Achilles' doom
and yet you live and love and are content
because the worst is known and much is good,
many would take your fortune if they could
and rise like stars into the firmament.
And as a boy your son wins every race
and every fight. You hide him as a maid.
Odysseus tricks him and he takes a blade
and not a spindle. No hair on his face,
never a line. He'll not live long enough
but will kill more than most. Rivers of Troy
run blood red from the victims of this boy.
The whole war pauses when he's in a huff.
When it is harvest and the sickles reap,
stalk after stalk is cut, falls to the ground.
Trojans and Amazons without a sound
fall to his sword and their companions weep.
Widows of men he's killed admire his skill.
Avenges lover cousin. Furious
dishonours killer's corpse. Magnanimous
comforts King Priam. And is hard to kill.
Your magic works a while. But then he dies,
a poisoned arrow takes his life away,
the victory's Agamemnon's. Bloody day,
fire-blackened towers are taken by surprise
and not by valour. This the final act
that will bring winds, speed the departing host
after ten years of war to ease his ghost.
Young princess' head is from her shoulders hacked.
Polyxena. The evening star's on high.
Bright Hesperus. And now fold back the sheet,

plump up the pillows. Consummation sweet
awaits the bride and groom. She with a sigh
welcomes him in. He proves up to his task
and they'll be happy now and always. Dawn
will soothe their sleep. In nine months' time is born
a son. Of course. You did not need to ask,
fond mothers fathers of the happy pair,
for all is known and every thread is spun
we'll weave it into patterns. Anyone
we show our tapestry will see it there."
And thus it was when gods walked among men.
The Fates would tell a bride her destiny
in between courses. But then piety
prevailed. Such things will not occur again.
A thousand cattle slaughtered in a day
on blazing altars. Jupiter would deign
to come to temples. For an hour remain
and talk or walk to town. When men would pray
Apollo and the Muses always came,
brought inspiration. On the field of war
Mars and Athena wallowing in gore
would lead another charge. It is a shame
we are no longer worthy. Civil strife;
brothers kill brothers; fathers poison sons
to fuck their widows; mother's anyone's
who'll take her. Murder is a fact of life,
rape incest and abuse in every home,
our piety is nothing but pretence.
Entirely forfeiting their confidence
the disapproving gods abandon Rome.

65.

I cannot write a word; they have all fled
from me, Hortalus, and the muses too.
My pain's a maelstrom. My thoughts batter through
like stormy waves at sea. My brother's dead.

An eddy out of Hell's dark river caught
his foot and tugged him. He was far from me
by Troy's wrecked walls, Rhoeteum's promontory,
dragged from our sight. I cannot bear the thought

I'll not see him again, yet love will last
and memory will bring him back. I'll long
to see him, and I'll mourn him in my song,
as sad as Procne, haunted by her past,

who, nightingaled, sang for the much-loved son
she killed, cooked, served her husband in a bun.

Meanwhile though, I must send you back your book.
I'm feeling guilty. All this meant I took

ages to read Callimachus. My mind
was elsewhere but your verses brought me back.
A good translation's something we all lack,
that you have given us. In it I find

this tale of absent-mindedness. A boy
gives his sweetheart an apple that she hides
inside her dress, and suddenly it slides
from where she left it, when she jumps for joy

seeing her mum come home, but what a shame!
the apple falls, she trips. Her mother knows
she got it from the boy. A huge row blows
up and forgetfulness is all to blame.

66.

He scanned vast darkness. In the sky at night,
so many things to watch, planets and stars
rising and setting, how a dark spot mars
the blazing sun. The rhythm of their flight
by hours and days the same, Conon could know
by watching. Yet love can draw down the moon
for young Endymion and may come soon,
or late, or any time. He saw me glow
new in the heavens, a bright lock of hair
from Berenice's head. Outstretched her arms,
asking that they might save him from all harms,
all of the goddesses that hear her prayer.
Her husband-king had gone off to the war
love bites and scratches up and down his back.
He goes to Syria and to Iraq
fresh from their wedding bed. She's sweetly sore.
Fathers, don't trust the wailings of the bride.
Nor, mothers, show concern for all their tears.
Custom dictates. It's not as it appears.
She stretches happy. And the gods all sighed
at her duplicity. I disapprove.
I know her better. Not the empty bed
lying alone, but fear that he was dead,
her king her brother-husband and her love,
this made her weep and sometimes she'd fall down
fainting from sorrow. Not how she'd behave
when younger. As a child she was so brave,
flirting and charming till she won her crown

when others did not dare. But oh her grief
saying farewell. She wiped away a tear
so often. Eros taught her how to fear
loss of her husband's body. Love's a thief
will steal us from our self. She promised me
with many oaths. A bull paid with his blood,
she sacrificed to every god she could
remember that he'd come back over sea
a victor and alive. Soon came that day.
Of joy—not mine. He made a swift return,
wore all the laurel crowns a man could earn
and added Asian lands to Egypt's sway.
Sad day for me, so promised. Then I left
her lovely head. It was against my will.
If I could have my way I'd grow there still.
But scissors conquered and I fell bereft.
Great mountains fall that almost hid the sun.
New seas appear. These things alone are real.
Fleets armies picks and spades and mighty steel
that severs all. Weaker than anyone
I fell. I curse the day men first found ore,
dug it out, smelted, later dug a pit,
poured it and shaped it and then hammered it.
Smoke darkened peoples of the Black Sea shore.
My sisters mourned my loss arranged in tiers
upon her head with combs. I lay in state
in Queen Arsinoe's shrine, a feather's weight,
Soft Zephyr son of Dawn that night appears,
bears me aloft a fluttering wingborn steed.
Venus who honours lovers honoured me,
stroked me. I lay there coiled upon her knee.

They honoured me. The goddess saw the need,
lest Ariadne's veil should shine alone,
tribute to lovers and fidelity,
our mistresses both blonde. She placed me there
still damp—the westwind brushed me through a wave—
and as the new girl learned how stars behave,
hung near the maid the lion and the bear,
Callisto, werewolf's daughter. And her son
who limps behind her cannot overtake,
for Juno hobbled him for vengeance sake.
I sink into the ocean as the sun
first shines on seafoam. Oh, be kind to me,
Nemesis punisher of sinful pride,
and stars don't pinch me just because I cried
on my first night. I knew I'd rather be
back on my mistress' head, perfume and oil
anointed, servants-twisted as a coil,
or loose, a little girl's hair wild and free.
Good wives, who were betrothed and now are true
to every marriage vow, and wait at night.
Your husband sees you naked with delight,
tears veils and sheets aside to come to you.
Do not forget me. Look into the sky
and make libation. You know what to do.
A good conditioner but first shampoo ...
I spit on gifts from women who defy
their vows, I scorn the perfume that they pour
and leave unworthy offerings in the dust,
adulteresses who are slaves of lust.
But on you wives who honour Hymen's law
blessings and harmony. But O my queen

honour Queen Venus and remember me
looking into the night. There you can see
me shining bright as I have always been
when yours. I'd rather not be star at all.
Let constellations jangle out of tune,
Orion's belt get wrapped around the moon.
To be your hair again, let Heaven fall.

67.

They say you were the nicest of all doors,
family-friendly, while that nice old man
was master here ... but when he died began
change for the worse (which everyone abhors)
and disrespect his son. What do you say?
—It's not my fault. Door's always get the blame.
Open and shut. They give us the bad name
belongs elsewhere. I say nay and thrice nay.
I'm just a door, stuck swinging on a hinge.
—So prove your innocence. —What kind of stuff
would make you see I'm speaking truth? —Enough!
Spill all the dirt you know and do not whinge.
—The bride was not a virgin when she came
into this house. Her husband's tiny prick
drooped like a parboiled bean and never rose
to the occasion or disturbed his clothes.
His father though made up for it. His dick
was there to do the honours in her bed,
whether he acted from incestuous lust
or just to get an heir did what one must.
His son could not perform. He did instead.
—Oh noble Roman! Oh such piety!
Pissed on son's honour! Ripped the veil
from his new daughter's face and made her wail
with pleasure all night long. —You can't blame me.
But wait, there's more. Brescia tells me so,
Mother of my Verona, best of towns,
with such good gossip too. Where bright dawn crowns

the hills, makes golden rivers as they flow.
She fucked Cornelius and as well
Postumius. —So, Door, how do you know
all of this when you only ever go
Open and shut and open? Kindly tell.
—She whispers to her servants in the hall.
And does not know that I can speak and hear,
doesn't drop hints but names her lovers clear.
Also red eye-browed Rufus comes to call.
Don't pass this on. Because he's scary mad,
recently sued over paternity
over the girl we know's fake pregnancy,
and nearly had to pay up handsomely
until she was delivered of a pad!

68.

I got your letter. It was soaked in tears,
short as it was ... You're such a wreck, you sleep
in cold chaste sheets and only wake to weep.
Awake in nights of grief that feel like years.
Venus would help you but she cannot reach.
You're lost in grief in waves like stormy sea
and in your anguish you have turned to me.
Though other greater poets cannot teach
you to survive, I'll try. Stand in their place.
I serve Her and the Muses. They will send
help to protect and save my host and friend.
I'm here. Be warned from wet tears on my face
I suffer too. You know, when I was young,
I played at sorrow. Sweet love and its cares
were all I thought of. As a young man wears
first adult clothes, the name of lover hung
not quite yet fitting, loose. Yet Venus, kind
to those who worship at her fleshly shrine
encouraged me. The songs I wrote were fine,
but now real grief enfolds, makes dark my mind.
My brother's dead. That fact tears all away.
My poems do not matter. They're a game
I played. And all my love affairs the same.
I want to help but really have to say
I'm weeping in Verona. I'm at home.
Where else to mourn? I lie in bed alone,
I do not care there's no one here to hold,
grief gnaws my limbs as much as aching cold.

I left all of my manuscripts in Rome.
I owe you much. My duty as a friend
to give you what you need, amusing stuff
that lightens burdens somewhat. Not enough,
but I have nothing here that I can send
but this which isn't going to be fun,
yet celebrates how much I'm in your debt,
tells future generations, to forget
your name would be a crime. So everyone—
Allius Manius was the best of men
so wipe the spiderwebs from off his tomb
if you should pass. Spare him our common doom,
oblivion. When love had made me burn
like Etna or the Hot Gates red at night,
eyes so cried-out I'd hardly any sight
and hollow cheeks—or when, mid flower and fern,
wetness, a spring, a quiet splashing stream,
swift through a town, a pool beside the road,
a traveller sweating, parched, a heavy load,
finds it and drinks as welcome as a dream
of gentle winds to sailors tempest-tossed—
he was the friend in need to our desire
our storm our burden our consuming fire—
he answered prayers, our Twins, when we were lost.
In his apartment anxious as a bride
I waited for her footstep in the hall,
her squeaky shoe. My Lesbia gave me all.
The coast was clear. Discreet she slipped inside.
We loved. She left. Soon there was nothing more.
Like Laodamia in Homer's song
one night of married love which seemed so long.

Her husband went off to the Trojan war.
First slaughtered there. While love is going on,
other things happen. Caesar. Helen. Blood
and weapons. And the tide was in full flood,
wind caught fleet's sail. And so soon love is gone,
trapped in Fate's gears. Abandoned for the war,
she never knew how bliss comes when you hold
your lover like a duvet in the cold
of winter. Greeks flocked, teemed, to Trojan shore.
So many died there. Troy itself then fell,
all slain by their adulterous desire,
Helen and Paris. One vast funeral pyre,
one grave, and now my brother's there as well.
His grave the end of joy for all our kin.
Pleasure and smiles and games that nevermore
delight. O Troy I loathe your fatal shore.
While Paris wallowed in their bed of sin
with Helen, angry Greeks cast home aside,
their wives unkissed. Among their tears the moan
of Laodamia in bed alone,
her marriage over that poor one night bride.
First love can overwhelm you, bear away
fierce rapids over rocks that foam and swirl,
out of control you're tossed around, poor girl,
feel awful sadness in the light of day.
It's like the river bore you underground.
In Thessaly flash mountain floods, cold, harsh,
gouged out the borders of a stinking marsh
where Hercules the mighty shelter found.
Dug deep, bided his time, then took his bow,
shot thirty times. His keen aim never erred,

each arrow took an iron-feathered bird
foul as a buzzards clever as a crow.
The labours that his master had imposed,
and after all his last reward was this:
apotheosis and maid Hebe's kiss.
After love's earnest work she stretched then dozed,
her duty done. Such joys as mothers know
who bear a son at last and do not fail.
The property is caught in an entail.
Grandfather's joy before he goes below
to see his lands go to a rightful heir,
her son. It cheers the old man's painful days
to disappoint a cousin's vulture gaze ...
a white cock pigeon tumbling through the air,
to tread his fancy mate knows such delight,
although she pecks so many other beaks
when he flies off. Most chaste of all the Greeks
was Laodamia alone at night,
happy in virtue. As my Lesbia fair
was not although more beautiful. He'd dance
attendance on her Cupid in a trance,
his own dart pierced him. She's beyond compare.
So many of us ask for nothing more
than share her favour, get a night alone,
kisses at least. Sometimes to hear her moan
in bed. Important not to be a bore.
The goddess Juno not known to complain
about her husband putting it about.
Gods will be Gods. I cannot do without
my love. And so I share Queen June's pain,
if man can goddess's. There were no rites.

No incense, and no father gave away,
never her husband. On her wedding day
I was not there. But she comes round at nights
if I am lucky ... that's a special time.
A private place has customs, little games,
we call each other special lover names.
When she has gone I put it into rhyme
for you my friend. I've done the best I can
to cheer you. Clear your name from filth and such.
It's not enough because I owe you much.
In times gone by gods would reward a man
did so much good. Themis the titaness
weighed out rewards for virtue. May they come
again, such times, and bring your house the sum
of happiness deserved and nothing less.
The house where we made love—long may it thrive.
Source of my luck. I love so much, it's clear,
dearest of all she is, dearer than dear.
My life's great blessing is she is alive.

69.

Don't be surprised, Rufus, if women all
refuse to let you bounce upon their thighs,
even when you offer life-time supplies
of the best kind of silks, the ones that fall

languidly to the ground, or precious stones
that glitter like the stars. They turn you down.
There is a rumour going round the town
that they've all heard—they feel it in their bones

disgust and fear of that huge billygoat,
the smelly one that lives beneath your arms—
foul breath, sharp horns. He really has no charms
for anyone who'd fuck you. And his coat

shows shaggy there, so wash and scent today
or please stop asking why girls run away.

70.

My love says that she would rather be
in my bed than in Jupiter's, but we
know that hot passion makes all women say
words carved in water and then washed away.

71.

His armpits stink; he also has the gout.
When they are making love, he is in pain
with every thrust. She has an angry pout
from smelling him. I'd have to be insane
not to enjoy this. They betrayed me. I'm
glad that they're also having a bad time.

73.

Give up on people—they are no damned good.
Don't expect anything but spite and gall.
Any kind deed is doomed. Folk really would
prefer to punish you for them. Of all
those I've been good to, he's my harshest foe
who says that he's my friend, and loves me so.

74.

Your uncle ought to tell you what is bad
and what is right. But one night Gellius had
his aunt. His uncle never said a word
for fear. And since, whatever has occurred,
keeps his mouth shut. Unless it's wrapped around
Gellius' dick, he doesn't make a sound.

75.

My mind's disturbed, my love, and you're to blame;
I cannot think straight and am caught in shame;
when you are good to me, I think you're cursed
and I still love you when you do your worst.

76.

What little pleasure I can take from these—
good deeds I did, and contracts that I kept,
oaths that I honoured—all these memories,
now stands me in good stead. I may have wept

all of this time over unhappy love
but there's much more to life. I may live long
years still. It's known before the gods above
I've injured no-one and done nothing wrong.

I trusted her; and she betrayed me; that
has wounded me near death. I've had enough.
I need to change my heart; the griefs that sat
there crushing me must go. It may be tough

to lay aside long love; it has to be.
I have to do it. It's my only chance
to regain health, to keep my sanity.
I have to end this poisonous romance,

whether I can or not. I need your aid,
gods, if you ever help men at death's door,
pity me now. I'm desperate, afraid
of what this love will do. I have no more

to say than, I've been good. It is unkind
that I feel love that's turned to a disease
that paralyses limbs and eats my mind.
Oh gods, have mercy. Stop me loving please.

I don't ask you to get me back her love,
to change her to a virgin from a bawd.
I want my health, I want you to remove
my love. I ask it as good deeds' reward.

77.

Rufus, my friend, I loved you, but in vain.
Not just in vain but also at the price
of feeling all my guts clamped in a vice
or something tearing out of them. Such pain
when poison's burning all your flesh away.
That's how it feels when your good friends betray.

78.

The best of uncles—helps his nephew bed
his brother's pretty wife and somehow can't
see, once the boy gets bored with one cute aunt,
he will seduce Gallus's wife instead.

78b.

I'm sad to see a smear of your foul spit
upon her lips. She's really not to blame.
You'll pay. I will immortalise your name.
Posterity will know you for a shit.

79.

Her brother's pretty. She would sacrifice
you and your family for just one kiss.
He's worse. He'd sell you at a knock-down price
—a few men's votes. And the sad truth is this.

80.

Most of the time your lips are ruby red,
Gellius, but then they're sort of flaky white,
a milk moustache when you're out late at night
or if you've spent the afternoon in bed
sharing a nap. There's gossip going round
that you suck lots of dicks. And don't wipe clean,
like a memento of just where you've been
with whom. All the penises you've found
neatly tucked under togas. While at home
poor little Victor is sitting alone
stirring a stockpot with a single bone
you galivant with half the men in Rome.
He strains to come and can't and wants to cry,
poor chap, you broke his balls and sucked them dry.

81.

There are so many handsome men around.
You could do better than the one you've found.
He's yellow, smells. Appropriately enough
he's from Pesaro. He's the one you love,
with whom you do all sorts of things in bed.
You could do better—e.g. me—instead.

82.

Quintus, I'm sure you would despise
some thief who with a scalpel pries
the eyes from someone's head. Surprise!
You are that thief. There's things I prize
more than my life, my heart, my eyes.
And you took that. With all your lies.
You pried my eyes.
Or what I prize
more than my eyes.
What a surprise
you told the lies and are the thing that you despise.

83.

Lesbia slags me off. Her foolish guy
enjoys her malice. It's at my expense.
"Catullus ... this and that." There is no sense
in his delight, and I will tell you why.

She bitches at me. She is still obsessed
with me, lusts for me. If she only could
shut up about it, then perhaps she would
forget our love and let the matter rest.

84.

'Arry 'as 'is own langwidge. 'E will say
"an hambush" for example, and look proud,
sure that 'e 'as it right. Will say things loud
and say 'em at each hoppurtunitay.
I blame 'is kin. 'is nuncle, first one freed,
'is muvver and 'is sisters and 'is aunt
vey all try to speak proper and they can't.
Are sure vey've got it right. Ho yes hindeed.
But now that he's gone East for good, our ears
are gently soothed by accents smooth and mild.
No more his mispronunciations wild ...
until a sudden thought brings back worse fears.
What if his accent spreads, so that one day
e'll sail back 'ome on the Hionian Say?

85.

I hate I love
and what the fuck? you say.
Dunno. That's how I feel,
torn into bits.

86.

I will admit that Quintia is tall,
quite shapely and with pale translucent skin.
There's many think she's beautiful. I'm in
a smaller group who don't think that all.
True beauty is not ticked off on a list
of single attributes. She's such a klutz
and doesn't get my jokes, which means she's nuts.
I'm sure there's other glaring faults I've missed.
Her good points don't add up to beauty. Sad
but there it is. My standards are quite high.
One woman's always there in my mind's eye,
who steals from other women what they had
by way of looks. They really can't compare
to Lesbia, even when she isn't there.

87.

I loved her more than any woman can
say she's been loved by any other man.
The vows of love that Lesbia and I made,
it was not I who broke them, or betrayed.

88.

He thrusts astride them, dinner through to dawn,
mother and sisters, and he makes them lick
his large excessively incestuous dick,
their clothes ripped off and all the bedsheets torn.
Of course it's not just after them he pants.
He pulled his uncle from a bridal bed,
he slapped him silly and then gave him head,
fucked second cousins and three maiden aunts.
There's no forgiveness he could ever get.
Not Oceanus the ruler of seas all
nor Tethys with her world-edge waterfall
could wash him clean or even make him wet.
He's practising a swivel of the hips
to get a blow job from his own sweet lips.

89.

He's so much slighter than you'd ever guess.
Why not? His mum's the apple of his eye
Such healthy lives—she never bakes a pie
too fattening. His sister's more or less
a health freak too. The uncle's really fit.
Works out a lot, though never at the gym,
and mostly it's the weight that presses him.
So nice to see a family closely knit.
Third cousins, nieces, the adopted brat
grandma acquired while on a trip to France,
half-naked nephews wrestling half-dressed aunts
This fitness kick is rather more than that.
Incest's the vice that really keeps them thin.
They've lost the taste for anything but sin.

90.

They're always at it, Gellius and his mum.
So let some magus from their fucking come,
redeem their sin. It's awful if it's true
but that is what they say the Persians do
to make the priests who hymn the sacred flame.
And get away with incest with no shame.
Their child will sacrifice to Jove each day
gut fat that like their guilt just melts away.

91.

I really was an idiot to trust
someone I know to be obsessed with sin
around my love. I thought, she's not his kin
and so she's not a target for his lust.
I'm mad for love of her, that's my excuse.
So mad I somehow thought that she'd be safe,
forgot he's one whom all restrictions chafe,
thought he was bound by friendship who's so loose
normal considerations don't apply.
I burn for her with such intense desire,
my commonsense consumed in raging fire
He reassured me, did not even lie.
"I love her like a sister." Should have known
that meant she's on his list of girls to bone.

92.

Lesbia can't shut up. I am so vile,
she says. I guess that means she loves me still.
And so I go on living. All this while
I love her and aloud I wish her ill.
That's how it works, will work until our death.
We love, but curse each other with each breath.

93.

You're noone up to whom I care to suck.
Caesar—good man or bad? Don't give a fuck.

94.

Big Dick fucks. Fucks a lot. It's not a shock.
His name has made him into one vast cock.
Each spice you cook gives flavour to your wok.

95.

Nine years, dear Cinna, and it's worth the wait.
Your tenants brought rich harvests in nine times.
Nine winters froze. Yet 'Smyrna' isn't late ...
Hortensius wrote fifty thousand rhymes
in those nine years. In far off years and climes
they'll read you. While his work will dissipate
forgotten; all those pages used to wrap
cat litter, fish and chips. It's all such crap.

96.

Perhaps salt tears taste sweet among the dead,
grief sounds soft music in their silent land—
so long since we were friends—I'll hold your hand.
Share mourning, yearning. Loves the years have shed
like leaves. She died so young, from Fate's harsh blow,
weep, and you bring her joy. Mourn her—she'll know.

97.

He stinks so bad, good gods, that I confuse
his arsehole and his mouth. Both so unclean
I hate to think just where they both have been.
An awful thought—if I were forced to choose

I'd have to kiss his arse. It doesn't bite.
With horse-sized rotting teeth and bleeding gums
or gape like some she-donkey's quim that comes
and drips. And yet he gets laid every night

or so he says. Perhaps he has some charm
for girls that I don't see. Gods, make him grind
yoked at some mill, nose stuck to her behind,
the she-ass. You, the cutie on his arm,

rather than have to kiss the likes of him
pick some blood-stinking torturer to rim!

98.

You snitch and stink. Your pompous lying tongue
rots in your mouth. Find better use for it,
there's many arseholes you could cleanse of shit
or lick a peasant's sandal free from dung.
Is hate the one idea left in your head?
Just yawn—the stench will leave us all for dead.

99.

I jumped on you and kissed you—honey kiss—
while you were concentrating on your game.
I made you angry—we've not been the same
since—you were harsh to me. Your anger is

like being crucified. You wiped your lips
as if they had been spat on by some whore,
as if you didn't want me any more
not any scrap or drop. Chased me with whips

as if you were a Fury. Your mouth's taste
on mine changed from the softest sweetness to
the bitterness of aloes, myrhh or rue.
I think we're done, and that is such a waste.

For if my kissing you caused so much pain
I won't hurt you by kissing you again.

100.

Loving as brothers, every time they meet.
One loves a boy twin, the other loves the girl.
Verona's small-town smart set in a whirl!
Caelius and Quintus—they are both quite sweet.
But if I had to choose, I won't be coy.
Love scorched me, turned the marrow in each bone
to wildfire. He was there. Caelius alone.
I hope he's lucky. Hope he gets his boy.

101.

To get here finally, I've had to fly
halfway around the world, and I've got here
too late for more than this. That's why I cry,
give you the gift I owe, a single tear

over your filled-in grave. We have no more
—our lucky grandparents believed so much
in ritual—and when disaster tore
people apart, they knew one day they'd touch

and souls would kiss. Standing around a grave
reading the words was just God's guarantee.
We don't believe. No ritual will save
our souls. And so I know I'll never see

you more. No hell or heaven when we die.
So, brother, I will greet you. Then goodbye.

102.

A feature of the best relationships,
Cornelius, is silent, loving trust.
The best are bound by this. I feel the same.
There is a god of silence in whose name
something is asked and quietly I must
go through with it, my finger on my lips.

103.

You've got ten thousand pounds I paid in fees.
Now pay it back, or mind your manners, please.
Be loud and rude, but at your own expense.
I hired you—and your manners cause offense
which, in your line of work, makes little sense.
I don't care if this makes me look a wimp.
I pay for better manners from a pimp.

104.

How can I curse my love, the one I prize
above all else, dearer than my own eyes?
One harsh vile word? One syllable thereof?
I can't; I am so deeply lost in love.
But you'll say what you want to put her down,
snarl like a monster, giggle like a clown.

105.

Big Dick thinks he's a poet—tries to climb
Parnassus. But the Muses throw him out
with pitchforks. Every poem is a crime
for which they prod him till they make him shout.

106.

That pretty boy now dates an auctioneer.
His price went up. To me he's very dear.

107.

The thing I hoped for, wanted most of all,
was something I could not expect to see.
I never thought that you'd come back to me
Lesbia. I never hoped that you would fall

back into love with me. I've yearned for this.
I'll celebrate this day of your return.
No man is happier. I've had to learn
through pain to treasure this most longed-for kiss.

108.

The people's hate will catch you when you're old
when vice has rotted you. I hear them say
tradition lays down punishments. I'm told
that first your vicious tongue gets carved away,
a buzzard's meal. Your eyes two ravens hold
a moment in their beaks then gulp. That day
your guts are a dog's dinner eaten cold
the other bits fierce wolves will drag away.

109.

Beloved, you're my life, so let's agree
that what we've got now lasts eternally.
You gods, stand as her good word's guarantee
that she speaks truly from the heart. Thus we
shake hands. It's peace and not a victory.
We'll live in bliss forever faithfully.

110.

Aufillena, there's girls I love and praise,
I give them presents and they come across,
put out a bit. I'm really at a loss.
It isn't fair at all. So many ways

you've got things out of me, so often teased
with hints you'd soon deliver and be nice.
It's a transaction and I've paid your price.
I hoped we had a deal, thought you were pleased.

Some girls are chaste, and that's all right with me,
they're not part of this game that we have played.
But rules are rules—you broke them, I'm afraid
that bit by bit you've sold your chastity.

Give me good value like an honest whore
and fuck me senseless. I'll respect you more.

111.

Aufillena, the best thing for a wife
is—love her husband truly all her life.
Or maybe simply put herself about,
for some have morals, some make do without.
To fuck your uncle—low as you can go!
Your son's the only cousin that you know.

113.

Pompey is diligent in his career.
Same consulate same Rome a different year.
His wife in her own way is just the same,
you know her, Nasal Drip Girl, wossername.
From one or two, it's now a street parade
of lovers. She works hard at getting laid,
pursues adultery at such high speed,
because she's swallowed gallons of his seed.

114.

I tell no lie—Big Dick's estate is vast.
Plump birds to trap on meadows lush and green,
there's other game and fish. His income's always been
less than expenditure. Gold flows so fast.

He is both rich and poor. Gives it to friends.
He's the Big Dick who spends and spends and spends.

115.

Big Dick has forty acres of green fields,
thirty of meadows. Quite a lot of marsh.
Not Croesus then, if we are being harsh.
Still it's rich land. He harvests what it yields.

And if his lands stretched to the Western Sea,
beyond the North Wind—forests, rivers, streams
all his, and wealth beyond his wildest dreams,
He'd not be changed by such prosperity,

in his erect colossal shade, we call
praise to his name, the Biggest Dick of all.

116.

I've tried to find a cool and tactful way
to get you off my case. Perhaps to send
Callimachus's works, just like a friend
would do. I've been obsessed with this all day.
His family were founders of Cyrene;
he conquered poetry. You'd like his stuff.
Perhaps. Though in your work you play so rough,
I know you've tried to stitch me up. I've seen
your verses whistle past me. And they miss
their target every time. You try in vain.
In vain I try to charm you. It's a pain.
Apparently you hate me. I'll say this.
About your satires I don't give a fuck.
Have some of mine. You'd better learn to duck.

AFTERWORD

Some years ago I got into an argument about whether there was, in the Classical world, a countercultural view that subverted the standard assumptions about penetration of inferiors and sexuality as subjugation, and suggested that Catullus was just such a more nuanced view. I started translating him to win the argument. Or rather, writing versions of his poems, based partly on my imperfect command of Latin but also an extensive reading of cribs.

I was also in the early stages of the exploration of traditional verse forms that became a feature of my return to poetry after thirty-five years of silence, and doing versions of Catullus became a way of improving technique in my own work.

I shall miss the entitled bitchy sentimental brilliant twerp I have come to know better than many of my acquaintances. I wonder what happened to him in the end—I fear nothing good. Like us. he lived in a world about to collapse into something rather different under the strain of its own contradictions.

My thanks are due to Jo Lindsay Walton for publishing this project, to Nick Lowe and Tony Keen for explaining some of the things I found difficult, and to John Crowley and Greg Feeley for their running commentary on these versions in social media.

Lightning Source UK Ltd.
Milton Keynes UK
UKHW021804301219
356125UK00003B/84/P